EDEN TWO-WAY

EDEN
Two-Way

by
CHAD WALSH

HARPER & BROTHERS
New York

EDEN TWO-WAY

FIRST EDITION

H-D

Library of Congress catalog card number: 54–9000

FOR EVA, MY WIFE

Kneeling against the window sill
We share a midnight and a hill.
And from the hill a road descends,
Flowing to where the midnight ends.
And from the road remembrance comes
Of any night of thicket plums
In flower, and any road where I
Have stood at midnight with the sky.
And since the thicket plums foretold
That I should kneel by you and hold
Your hand in mine, come, let us go
And see the road of midnight flow
Around the silver hill, and there
I shall pin blossoms in your hair.

ACKNOWLEDGMENTS

For painstaking and discerning criticism of this book while it was in preparation I am indebted to my good friends, Robert S. Jackson and Robert H. Glauber.

Grateful acknowledgment is made to the editors of the following magazines for permission to include here poems which first appeared in their publications:

A.D. for "The Meditation of the Roots" (No. 3 of "The Whirlpool Out of Time" in EDEN TWO-WAY)

The American Scholar for "The Theology of Hitchhiking" (No. 5 of "Twenty-Three Sonnets: Eros and Agapē")

The Beloit Poetry Journal for "Epithalamium for Bob and Jackie"

Epoch for "Suburban Vista"

Golden Goose for "Breathe Deeply, Plunge" (No. 23 of "Twenty-Three Sonnets: Eros and Agapē")

Ladies' Home Journal for "Any Night of Thicket Plums" (dedicatory poem)

The Living Church for "Descent into Hell" and "The Vertical Moment"

Poetry: A Magazine of Verse for "Elysian Fields, California"

Spirit: A Magazine of Poetry for "The Road to Stonehenge," "Spiritual Biography," "A Myth Is a Mode of

Seeing" (No. 1 of "Twenty-Three Sonnets: Eros and Agapē"), "When the Suns Expire of Pallor," (No. 17 of "Twenty-Three Sonnets: Eros and Agapē"), "The Alchemy of Light" (No. 21 of "Twenty-Three Sonnets: Eros and Agapē"), and "In Summer When the Woods Are Slow"

The University of Kansas City Review for "X-Ray Clinic" ("Mortal in the X-Ray Clinic") and "Planned Metamorphosis" (No. 18 of "Twenty-Three Sonnets: Eros and Agapē")

Voices for "The Lake of Our Love" (No. 22 of "Twenty-Three Sonnets: Eros and Agapē")

Certain of the poems listed above appear in revised form in the present work.

CONTENTS

The Ailanthus Tree   *1*

Christmas in the Straw   *4*

Descent into Hell   *5*

The Eden of Our Instants   *6*

Elysian Fields, California   *8*

Epithalamium for Bob and Jackie   *10*

For Marion Munford   *11*

The Golden Gate and Home   *12*

In a Time of Leaves Falling   *14*

In Summer When the Woods Are Slow   *15*

A Lament for Old Comrades   *16*

Love in Corte Madera, California   *17*

Mortal in the X-Ray Clinic   *18*

Nuptial Hymn   *19*

Our Days, Like Sodden Cheerios   *22*

Poem in Lieu of the Blessing of the Nuptial
  Ring   *24*

Public Figure   26

The Road to Stonehenge   27

The Secret Bower   28

The Serious Young Man in a Conservative Raincoat   29

The Snow Shovel   34

A Song for Willing Ghosts   37

Spiritual Biography   38

Suburban Vista   40

Talpa, New Mexico   41

Taos by Daylight   44

They Walk Under Ladders   45

Twenty-Three Sonnets: Eros and Agapē   46

   1   I thought it rather odd one rib was missing
   2   The sacramental trees in priestly spring
   3   All beds are preëxistent. Why should we
   4   The massacre of solar hydrogen
   5   Hitchhikers are justified by faith through grace
   6   Hide the broom in the rafters; your Dad's com-
          ing
   7   You do not grow Euclidian but stranger
   8   Earth we are of the earth. Then why not probe
   9   I should have been a pair of ragged claws

10   Return, return, and turn to me again
11   As a communicant, past accidents
12   We spat into the Yalu. Can you remember?
13   You are the contour map of God's creation
14   With God all things are possible. Poor dancers
15   As your light breath stirs and impedes my sleep
16   You dare not die before me. When you die
17   Shall I compare you to a marble plaque
18   When I am dead, mummify me no more
19   We cannot plead compatibility
20   When the unnatural warm fair October
21   I see you sitting in the easy chair
22   To the left, cliffs; the shore where cottages
23   After so many waves, after gray mountains

Unscientific Postscript   62

The Vertical Moment   63

When the World Drowned   64

The Whirlpool Out of Time   66
1   The Garden of Common Sense
2   Rain, Rain, Go Away
3   The Meditation of the Roots
4   A Place of Skulls
5   He Descended
6   The Song of the Sparrow
7   A Terrible Beauty Is Born

Geographical Note   75

EDEN TWO-WAY

THE AILANTHUS TREE

If you would understand, I must explain
The moment had no signboards for my notice;
There were the puddles from the slackening rain,
A sidestreet, one of any in the city,
Small, wooden houses, crowded, and the paint
    flaking.

There were the usual children, ragged and loud,
Watching the stranger. You have seen their faces
In Sunday supplements, when three more weeks
Till Christmas stirs the suburbs and the rich
To brief remembrance of the city alleys.

From upstairs windows, housewives shaking
    dustmops
Bellowed commands to children in the street;
The homeward men paused at the corner tavern,
Explored their pockets, jangled coins, and entered,
While others sauntered forth on sailors' feet.

And up one driveway, at the further end,
A lone ailanthus sprouted from the concrete

For twenty feet, it might be, in the air
Toward the reputed heaven of its name
Which otherwise had sown no ready symbols.

But most of all, I saw the surging children
Condemning random cars to second gear
And flowing round me in the casual eddy
That marks a small and unimportant reef
Encompassed by a sea with things to do.

My mind, a vagabond, turned choir director.
I clothed the boys in cottas crisp with starch,
And purple bow-ties ample as carnations;
Ranged them in rows, and listened as they chanted
What Gregory composed for Anglicans.

No mystery in this. The vagrant mind
(Supremely when the stomach longs for supper)
Creates a second world to speed the time;
Nor did I fuse the fancy with the fact—
A sidestreet, one of any in the city.

But suddenly the eddy round me straightened;
As though at an inaudible command,
The boys, twenty or thirty strong, streamed past me
In double file, flooded into the driveway
And two by two assailed the tree of heaven.

2

And two by two they reached the topmost branch
And would not stop. Without a sign they shinnied
Into the sky, still in a double file.
"Look out!" I yelled. They did not hear my warning,
For as I called to them, the gray sky opened,

Opened in a wide cleft of golden light,
And voices sang—I could not see the singers—
"Glory, glory, hallelujah." The boys
(The farthest ones were small and wholly golden)
Sang back in perfect plain song, "Glory, glory,"

Sang with voices fading at their ascent
Until they vanished in the golden glory
And the gray sky resumed its wonted rights,
Leaving for witness but a vague gold streak
Such as one sees on misty days at sunset.

I watched until the last of gold had faded
And then walked home to supper getting cold.
Months later I revisited the alley
One five o'clock, and saw no boys at play
Within the bracket three-to-seventeen.

That's how it stands. I don't recall, this moment,
The alley's name, but somewhere in my files
I know I have it. I can find it for you
If you are eager to investigate.
But I have told you everything I know.

CHRISTMAS IN THE STRAW

In heaven it's Allemande Left and Promenade
And Swing That Corner Lady One And All.
This is the music that the fiddler played
When stars danced out of nothing at his call.

This is the dance the fiddler danced when Eve
Danced to her feet from Adam's wounded side.
This is the song the fiddler sang at eve
Beside a cradle and his Jewish bride.

The angels sang the song the fiddler played.
The sheep and shepherds danced a Texas Star,
And wise men heard the music and obeyed;
The camels' feet kept rhythm with a star.

One and all, come this way.
Hear the fiddler sing and play.
Join your hands and form a ring,
Stamp your feet, dance and sing,
Hallelujah, now sashay!

DESCENT INTO HELL

True, I had read the sign above the gate—
Lasciate ogni . . . and I knew my Dante.
But I had packed so many words to hate
That time to parse the sign was rationed, scanty.
My first impressions were encouraging.
No neighbors called across the picket fence;
I never heard the rusty doorbell ring;
Time and the landscape stretched level, immense.

And I had time to be a Socrates
And know myself. With knowledge, ardor grew.
I could make love to me, and me gave teas
For I, and dried our tears. But who are you,
My silent enemy? O God, why do you wait,
Infinite sponge, draining my finite hate?

THE EDEN OF OUR INSTANTS

I suppose we all knew that Eden had been lost.
Certainly no roving photographer ever certified it for
Life,
And the reports of the explorers, though at first
encouraging,
At weary last ticketed Tibet and Polynesia with the
plagued lands of our feet.
But backward or forward, inward, outward or
upward,
With the drugs of self-transcendence we have sought
the lost world,
Like the children of bombed parents, mute beside
Korean wheel-ruts.

Eden has opened an instant in blank verse, in music,
in bed,
In the arms of a locust tree upon the strict sky,
In dreams joyfully surrealist, and we have cried,
"Halt!"
But flaming swords scorched our tongues into
smarting silence,

6

The nasty jokes of little boys drowned out the
    earnest of music,
The roving self returned to its derelict habitation,
Thorns and thistles separated the toes of our routed
    feet.

ELYSIAN FIELDS, CALIFORNIA

They died in Iowa or Nebraska. They had lived good
    lives.
Flying saucers swiftly bore them to the pastures of
    the blessed.
Death, like the slagheaps of the Rocky Mountains,
    delimits their republic.
They will never return to the flesh of the east, the
    snow of mortality,
The procession of the borning leaf, the green leaf,
    the bleeding leaf, the fallen.
Here no leaf twists in a last spiral to the cognate
    humus.
Here the laurel bush and the live oak brood on the
    pale green hills,
Hills the breasts of a twilight mother, not a midnight
    mistress,
Here the flowing fog tenderly makes vague the faces
    of the dim immortals,
Dido and Sychaeus hold hands beneath the acacia's
    golden currants,

Aeneas concludes his guided tour, assails the coastal range,
Sets sail westward, ever westward, on the blue, the dangerous, the living sea.

EPITHALAMIUM FOR BOB AND JACKIE

As the world quietly vaporized in a mist of white
    flowers
And organ music, you were atomized with it.
When its component parts reassembled in the valid
    pattern,
The pronouns of your egos swirled like atoms
And *we* recessionally was construed with a singular
    verb.

Stand on the mountain peak and trace the thin path
Twisting athwart the route markers of English 201
Past dangerous April nights and cliffs of music
And sands of separation. See the detours
At every turning, the lost paths you did not take.

Yours was the freedom to veto predestination,
To tangent off to the nowhere whose name is hell.
But in free necessity you walked by faith in the
    mystery,
The world is made new in the light and the might
    of the mystery,
And the mystery and you forever are one.

10

FOR MARION MUNFORD
confirmed in St. Stephen's Church

I was not there. I wish that I had been
To see the Holy Spirit settling in,
His purchase sealed by few words quietly said
And hands, holiness-gnarled, upon your head.
I was not there to see your Pentecost.
(Would I have seen them, seven flames, wind-tossed,
Like good Greeks each a bearer of a gift?)

Stephen beheld the helpless ceiling lift
And drift away, the heavens open wide,
Revealing Son and Father side by side.
Kneeling in Stephen's church, did you see too?

The mysteries, made sight and sound for you,
Are your privacy. I shall not intrude.
(I too have been remarked, pursued, and wooed.)

The Holy One, a frequent, friendly guest,
Entered the house that he had long possessed
In all but deed, arranged the bread and wine
And vowed the welcome home into his shrine.

THE GOLDEN GATE AND HOME

Fog descending
Day retreating
In a rout of surly starlings
Sea gulls eating
On the useless ferry pier
Fine rain beating
At the greyhound and the bus
Is it always thus
Here with us?
Here
Here and everywhere
Faces faint in fog rain riven air
What of us can lift above the mist
Like the top third of the tower
Hanging firm and rose
Held by no demonstrable power?
At the Sausalito stop
Briefly kissed
By the young man with the checkered tie
The reluctant girl with vague blond hair
Entered sat beside me

Circled in her solitude
I
Watched the gulls gregarious at food
While the window drained the gray Pacific
Drop by drop

IN A TIME OF LEAVES FALLING

The snow will fall and fell the twigs.
Late autumn is a time of prigs,
The white of cold veracity
Dethroning all the golden wigs.

There is no elm or maple tree
That is not worse for honesty.
The gravepit black, the gravebones white
Radically paint the parody.

Then welcome back the artful green
And painted birds that proudly preen
Their feathers in the outer dress
Of limbs assumed but best not seen.

IN SUMMER WHEN THE WOODS ARE SLOW

In summer when the woods are slow
And rivers have no strength to flow,
We'll lie in shadows, face to face,
Divorced by half an inch of space,
My hands pacific at my side
Until the pointed shadows glide
In rippling arrows on the lake.

When faint winds chill the frogs awake,
My hands will stir with laissez-faire
And cautiously exploit your hair.
We'll rise, two shadows on a shore,
To see the bats circle and soar.

Divorce with us was civil and solar.
The hour is lunar and the polar
Whiteland retreats, pursued by flowers
Through our infinitude of hours.

A LAMENT FOR OLD COMRADES

What shall I do to bring them back?
They have gone into the black.

A menshevik and living yet
With the green things and the wet,

What shall I do for flesh and bone
Turned to meteoric stone?

For I have known them warm and weak,
Veins to bleed and lips to speak,

And now they circle with the spheres,
Crystal lips and rigid ears,

They move by laws of mass and space,
Vacant as a lunar face,

Too dead for death, in noons of black.
What will bring, who will sing, them back?

LOVE IN CORTE MADERA, CALIFORNIA

The oranges of light ripen for our guidance
In the fog. There are three lanes to wheel us home.
No stopping or turning, and forty-five. We shall
    arrive in good time,
Kindle a Presto log, pour muscatel, and schedule love.

Alcatraz blazed to the east, bright hell
Whence love is excluded by law. The devils and the
    damned
Inaudibly glared from windows of fire
At the Golden Gate moated by impassable currents.

The fireplace drowses into embers, and so to bed,
Ritual exact as the Canon of the Mass.
Your face beneath me inherits, through a mile of fog,
The purgatorial glow of San Quentin, filtered for
    love.

MORTAL IN THE X-RAY CLINIC

This fluttering machine that the buzzing X-ray probes
Like an apprentice wiretapper in Hoover's FBI
Undresses for Sibyl and Virgil the prophesier
To hear the particular death that it shall die.

The graying lady in black releases the film;
Nodding shared sadness, she glides from the radiant
     room
To engrave in darkness and chemically measured
     moments
The black and silver ordnance map of doom.

I look from the window; the snow is deep and silver;
Two lovers confirm their map on flashing skis,
And I only can see, paler than gray, the two agents
That shadow them from between the blackly carious
     trees.

NUPTIAL HYMN

You have wished to be alone together. Well, you
    have your wish.
After the spiked punch, the cake, the hired
    photographer,
After the screeching horn that proclaimed you
    through the city,
Here is the cottage, the week's rent is paid, the lake
    laps softly.
Darkness has come very soon. In one of your
    suitcases
Society's benediction and the Church's nihil obstat
    leer encouragingly,
Signed by witnesses and minister. This cottage is your
    castle.
If you took off all your clothes, and she took off
    hers, too,
And someone by strange chance entered, it would be
    you who phoned the police.
All the formalities are correct; the final formality is
    legal.

How very black the night is. Walk outside with her.

If other human beings share the world, their
     existence is an exercise of faith.
A cricket chirps in a low, reedy hum. A few leaves
     rustle.
The stars by their very brightness neon the fact of
     night. Time passes.

When you find her in bed, in the timorous moment
Before you turn off the light in the adjoining
     bathroom,
When you see her at last, as different as panther
     from a tiger,
Alien firmness and three-dimensioned lines in the
     swift night,
There is still time, time before the irreparable
     violence,
Time before you are lost and she is teased into
     moaning dependence—

There is still time. Not now the quick rush of the
     blood,
The easy lewdness of the mind when at fifteen
You collected pictures of girls in bathing suits.
There is still time before you commit the sober
     violence
That is the lingua franca, the Esperanto of the
     panther and the tiger.

20

There is still time. It is perfectly possible and legal
For you to remember a book, half read, due back at
the library in the morning,
Or you have forgotten to buy a birthday present for
your mother,
Or you must fill out in triplicate a questionnaire from
a testing bureau.
She, for her part, can with a simple headache, natural
epiphenomenon of over-excitement,
Offer you a peaceful reprieve, and a night's sleep
while the lake laps softly.

If she is a wife in the morning, let it not be your
boasting.
Violent giver, the violence was the gift of the good
Lord God, the sensuous,
Who in prevision of your two decades of
unproductive behavior patterns,
Plotted before the foundations of the world were
laid
His counter-measures to pacify your quibbling and
niggardly mind.
Go to bed. The God of the paramecium and
nemathelminth will goad your complex
evolution.

OUR DAYS, LIKE SODDEN CHEERIOS

Our days, like sodden Cheerios, hang on a string.
Lord have mercy upon us.
The Bay surges in low ruffles to the slanting rain.
San Quentin is faint as the Celtic past.
Tamalpais crouches decapitated by descending fog.
Domine miserere.

In the Muir Woods the impassive redwoods grow,
Middle-aged with Henry VIII, young with the schism
     of Rome and Constantinople.
The fronds of their leaves droop nourishing rain to
     the feeding roots.
They will die and they do not know it.
The creek of life surges with pale green gold
     amongst them.

We wear, and we know it, the cold, wet necklace of
     time and death.
Christe miserere.
Tamalpais is the rumor now of a rumored race.
The Bay flows in short surges, but not for us.
Domine miserere.

In thee have I trusted.
Let me never be confounded.
In manus tuas
Commendo spiritum meum.

POEM IN LIEU OF THE BLESSING OF THE NUPTIAL RING

Then let us sing. The ring your finger wears,
Though dedicated by no formal prayers,
Encircles in fee-simple lands as vast
As God's plural estates. I am aghast
At how great a transfer of rights was this
And how lightly we sealed it with a kiss
Slight as the beads that stealthily bought Manhattan.
The title is in English, not in Latin.
These rites were rights. And I, the pioneer,
Braving the trees and Indians with fear
Matched, have achieved some clearings in the woods
And a stockade to guard my house and goods.

But when I venture out with yoke and plow,
There on the forest fringe a twitching bough
Betokens Indians lurking—or a bird
Alighting. Can I know? And I have heard
By night far screams, and a steady drum beating.
I am not sure the forest is retreating.

All this was listed in the deed of sale.

One cannot buy cosmology and fail
To find attached some clauses in fine print.
The lawyer dropped more than a passing hint.
God has (God knows) a purpose for dark trees,
For bobcats, bears, and painted savages,
Though what it is, I cannot understand.
I plow and plant and reap in the cleared land.

Well, let me yoke the team, open the gate.
I think too much. The season's turning late.
And if the woods scream, load your gun and wait.

PUBLIC FIGURE

He hardly knew just when the Boswells came,
And they all kept their pencils out of sight.
The living room was visibly the same,
And he, but for some scattered hairs now white.

Talk was as usual, he did not mean
To tailor sentences, half written, spoken.
There were only the hushes wedged between
His first phrase and the second to betoken

The loss of innocence. And he resisted
The sack of Eden and eviction papers
By owlish listening, or answers twisted
Into pure nonsense, and verbal capers.

But sighing he heard at last posterity's pencil
And learned to speak as one types a ditto stencil.

THE ROAD TO STONEHENGE

I walked between the poppied wheat
And saw the circling beeches meet
In Druid clusters on the plain,
The air aslant with almost rain.

From Amesbury the pale road weaves,
Armored with rigid hawthorn leaves
Against the unredeemed arrears
Of lightly dozing heathen years.

Jerusalem here is far and thin,
No deeper than the fragile skin
Of topsoil lapsing to the sea
To set the chalk and old gods free.

The neopagan sky tilts low,
The lorries have no place to go,
The upper terror and the nether
Meet in gray slants and lean together.

The earth more restless than the sky,
The dead more living now than I,
The road a frail and winding thread
Between the resurrecting dead.

THE SECRET BOWER

After the gadgets and the badgered hours,
After a space and spate of potted flowers,
We set about constructing secret bowers.

We built for them a climate with no snow.
They had to be as guileless as Rousseau.
That's why construction work was very slow.

But build we did, without a hardware nail,
One bower permitted to each proper dale.
The postman did not find us with the mail.

You were the altar laid to Amor Rex.
Our lips were innocent of sin and sex.
And neither Freud nor Jesus came to hex.

Above each bower above each mating pair
The good birds sang like angels in the air.
I plaited blue spring daisies in your hair.

A summer's worth the bower that we shared
Was summer strong. Fall flared and winter glared.
I wonder how the other settlers fared.

THE SERIOUS YOUNG MAN IN A
CONSERVATIVE RAINCOAT

A serious young man in a conservative raincoat stands
By my side; I do not think he came through the
    receiving line,
And I rather suspect, from the small black notebook
    in which he is writing shorthand,
That he is a man under orders to a master whose
    identity I have not established.
It is very difficult to discuss Matisse with the lady
    now moving through the line.

I was duly confirmed. Only the most perfunctory
    questions were asked.
There was little opposition and less interest when I
    was sent on my mission.
But afterthoughts are always easier than forethought,
    ex post facto dubiety.
The Minister of Cults would choose this moment to
    summarize his thesis on Hegel.
I could ask him, the young man, I mean, his name
    and whether he wishes a private interview,

But that in itself is a confession of guilt and also
    implies
An official familiarity with his functions—and
    officially he is not here at all.

The Roumanian chargé d'affaires is very tedious when
    he talks Hemingway and Erskine Caldwell.
This question of guilt troubles me; I am semantically
    becalmed.
If some day, and it may be soon, I receive a message
    in the most secure code,
Recalling me from my mission for testimony, I am
    not sure what I shall say.
In that court, if it is a court,
Whatever I say will be held against me.
At least I have never heard of a verdict of innocent,
And the rare instances of "not proven" never seem
    to restore the status quo ante.
He has put his black notebook in his raincoat pocket
    and is pulling out another.

It is not that my conscience convicts me, but neither
    does it exonerate.
And how is a conscience, itself a party to the facts,
    to sit enthroned in aloof judgment?

Perhaps I should welcome an objective evaluation
    and verdict,
The catharsis of bowing my head in acquiescence to
    the TV cameras,
The multitudinous invisible jury of the people's court.

This fool—what is his name?—in the movie usher's
    uniform—
Some minor minister, I presume—is using me as his
    Berlitz tutor—
But I must be polite.
What was I saying?
TV? Guilt? Conscience? The young man?
TV—yes. I was saying, or almost ready to say,
There is a cleansing power in TV. One should rejoice
    in its invention.
For I have been guilty, guilty from birth. Not
    precisely guilty
Of the charges that this young man's master is most
    likely arraigning against me,
But looking at it more broadly, my guilt is
    incontestable,
Though I am quite unable to put it into the words
    of a formal confession,
And the experts have tried to persuade me that fewer

clothes or a semester of semantics would cleanse
    me
Of the illusion of guilt.
But if my guilt is illusion,
I am illusion;
Therefore I choose to affirm my guilt
Though, as I say, I cannot specify—
C'est un grand plaisir, es ist ein grosse Freude, sehr
    reizend.

Young man (I shall think the words) you look
    almost stupid,
Standing there, so dutifully writing Gregg shorthand
    in a little book.
Your master, is he as stupid as you?
It is very probable. And the people's court will be
    most stupid of all—
Gawking mouths, mouthing tags and rags of
    barbershop political philosophy,
Heads wagging with the satisfied smirk of vindicated
    mediocrity.

So be it. Let me go down, down, let me be proved
    guilty,
And if the indictment—for such it actually is—
    specifies the wrong crimes,

So be it. Let me go down. I am guilty.

From the day of my birth the Siamese twin of my
     guilt has shared my heart and lungs.

If there is cleansing, any cleansing, in the white Klieg
     lights, the multitudinous invisible leering faces,

If from the surgery of the mob some mutilated life
     survives, grows, grows guiltless,

So be it.

I am damned and doomed. Let me be condemned.

Es freut mich sehr, Ihre Bekanntschaft zu machen.

     Young man,

In la tua voluntate sia mia pace.

THE SNOW SHOVEL

It is the first snow of the season, and I am walking
    home from Sears,
Balancing the big badge of my improvidence, 30
    inches wide, guaranteed kind to sedentary backs,
Light weight and expensive as the aluminum trust
    can make them.
The long hill that leads from the Methodist Church
    to the College observatory
Winds white before me; soon I shall be home, and
    the hundred feet of the driveway.

This is a time to ponder the philosophy of hard
    work, to plan a blank verse meditation
Lauding the life of simple toil, and the character
    built by moving snow three feet from where it
    fell,
And if the Puritan heritage that flows in all American
    veins,
Even those whose names end in *-ini, -ski,* and *-strom,*
Were not so sluggish in me this overcast day,
I would almost believe I believed it.

But the cost of the shovel and the angle of the hill
    and the length of the driveway
Impart to my mind today a cold biblical clarity; when
    my brow sweats, and the sweat quickly
    congeals,
I shall sing no songs of the nobility of work, but
    rather accept, with what meekness I can, the
    standard curse that Adam contrived for me
    without asking my leave.

I find it sometimes wonderfully refreshing to tell the
    truth. Not many people enjoy this luxury.
That is one of the reasons the Bible is more bought
    and admired and translated than read.
Let me continue and tell some more truth.

Paradise is a Polynesian island, precisely as the
    romantics have always known.
The fruit falls to the ground at the exact moment of
    ripeness, and the few yards of walking to pick
    it up are a pleasant stroll in the climate that is
    attached;
In paradise you eat fruit, write poetry, make love,
    and say your prayers,
Four activities, and almost the only four, that are
    self-validating;

This is the truth, but the other truth is that we do
    not live in paradise; we live in Wisconsin;
The white flakes of the ancient curse are new as
    today's *Beloit Daily News;*
I shall shovel the driveway, put the car to bed,
Read *The New Yorker,* play a folksong on the alto
    recorder, and retire from thinking.

A SONG FOR WILLING GHOSTS

So many falling stones have toppled down
Upon our heads, so many creeping things
With tentacles have occupied the town,
Existence is a verb and not a noun.

Sometimes we have no very certain proof
That we are not a pair of tardy ghosts
(Even the tentacles remain aloof)
Aiming at love beneath a vanished roof.

If we are ghosts, at any rate the stones
From broken cornices are innocent.
They cannot break our purely private bones;
The dying need not vex us with their groans.

Since there's no being sure, let's say we're dead,
And being dead, we've had our time of dying.
As carefree ghosts we share a haunted bed,
My specter hand can stroke your phantom head.

SPIRITUAL BIOGRAPHY

No sooner said or done, the word or deed,
Than memory mythologized it. He'd
Convey it safely to his room and test
It for the sins so subtle when confessed
They rang like virtues. Morning-after heads
And crude carnality of bouncing beds
Were not for him. He ate Augustine's pears
And classified their seeds in frequent prayers.
(Father O'Brien heard his voice with terror,
And ladled penances by trial and error.
"Sweet Mary, give me Micks that beat their wives,"
He said, "or Wops too free with carving knives.")

He died, he died. It was as he expected—
Not welcomed home nor finally rejected.
His stay in Purgatory lasted ages;
His monologues would fill ten thousand pages;
St. Peter's agents, whom he often met,
Invariably reported back, "Not yet."
The population ebbed and flowed, and he
Progressed in conscience and seniority

Until one day a spirit newly come,
And reeking still of nicotine and rum,
Told him a good one of a farmer's daughter.
He laughed. He paled. He laughed again. The water
Of clear humility rained down his skin,
Dissolved the lucent sheath of subtle sin.
(St. Peter's sides were aching when he let him in.)

SUBURBAN VISTA

Living as we did in one of the nicer suburbs
With an A & P next to the second stop-light,
Even a church for those who cared for such things,
We seldom had need to visit the historic city.

Dimly we remembered the cars advancing, receding
In the parallel veins and arteries of four-lane
    highways.
Delicatessens and department stores found the
    stop-light.
Perhaps as a child I went one time to the city.

We have had trouble-makers—collectors of folklore,
Waylayers of old men at the psychosomatic clinic,
Probers, explorers with knapsacks and Geiger
    counters,
Who strode down the grassy concrete to find a city.

Some of them stumbled home, to haunt us and tell us
How near they approached to the vitrified lawn
    where the statehouse
Stood. But our water and gas mains generally
    function,
And we hanged the alarmists high high from the
    vibrating stop-light.

TALPA, NEW MEXICO

"Buenas tardes," I said. "Buenas tardes," he replied,
As though my gaunt Saxon face were privileged to
    speak Spanish
Without the answering arch of an eyebrow.
They are kind in Talpa, and never surprised.

At the head of the little street, Señor Martínez
Offers apples at a reduced rate to his cousins and
    friends
(Anyone living this side of Ranchos).
The piñon fires in the vertical hearths
Send resinous pillars of smoke over the adobe roofs.
Down the road, toward Ranchos, on the right side,
The ashes of Talpa quietly return to ashes,
Memorialized by mounds of pebbles and wood
    crosses.

Across the street from our house is the adobe church,
Open when the Ranchos priest remembers to come.
The school children talk fiesta and piously play
    hooky.
From the irrigation ditch comes a music half water
    half willows,

And the sight of old women, gnarled as piñons,
    bending with buckets.
Every decent family paints the inner walls once a year
With *tierra blanca;* there are flower pots in the
    windows.
When it snows, all Talpa talks from the flat roofs,
As swishing brooms race against melting mud.

Girls of thirteen, giggling bilingually, go to the
    roadhouse,
Dance, and are disputed with knives; at sixteen they
    marry,
Or if they forget to marry and a lapse of memory is
    born,
No picture is turned to the fresh white wall; flesh is
    weak, Mary is patient;
Who can be sung into heaven without his quota of
    Masses?

They are kind in Talpa; Talpa is dying. The young
    men,
Remembering G.I. rations and three-day leaves,
Depart; they change your tires and check your
    carburetor
In Taos and Santa Fe. The girls work in the dime
    stores.

42

Back in Talpa, small children play with their
    grandparents.
The irrigation ditch is singing; the willows bend;
From the Sangre de Cristo Range the winds descend,
    bringing the ranks of snow
To scour and thicken the patient adobe roofs.

TAOS BY DAYLIGHT

Broken Spanish, where they talk it, drunken,
By the road that climbs to Taos out of Ranchos,
Madison, West Madison in Spanish,
Skid Row shrunken
To a trinity of taverns. El Crepúsculo will vanish,
Vanish utterly, gone the painters, poets
And the know-its
Know-it-alls.
Evening falls.
And the Indians draw their blankets closer,
Light their Camels, circumscribe the plaza,
Pueblo faces uncommitted as the moon.
Once a grocer,
Sane and Saxon,
With a wife and two sons flaxen,
Bought a store adobe style in Taos,
Built a Cape Cod house.

THEY WALK UNDER LADDERS

They walk under ladders and joke with black cats.
They knock on many doors but never on wood.
By preference they choose hotels with a thirteenth
    floor.
They beget 1.3 children per pair, and send it
To a progressive school where creativity is
    compulsory.
During the Easter holidays they recommend *The
    Golden Bough.*

They often remain married; they have sex twice a
    week;
They carry 20-40 insurance; they join the AAA.
Sometimes they wonder if Vedanta perhaps is the
    answer.

They publish their memoirs at the age of fifty-two.
They specify cremation or a cemetery with horizontal
    monuments.
They look at gray hairs in a broken mirror.
They read Gayelord Hauser; they eat yogurt;
The face in the mirror forgets to smile back.

TWENTY-THREE SONNETS:
EROS AND AGAPĒ

1

I thought it rather odd one rib was missing,
But then I'd lost a tooth the month before.
I saw no cupids fluttering and kissing.
You looked quite solid, standing on the floor.
And solid, solemn were our first remarks,
Gravely excited talk of worthy books;
We mourned for Spain between the city parks,
And civic issues by the purling brooks.

The surgeon of my sleep was skilled and wise.
He left no scar, no X to mark the spot.
He also operated on my eyes.
I looked and saw the light, a golden dot
That grew until my new eyes could perceive
Golden and firm the newly minted Eve.

2

The sacramental trees in priestly spring
Have transubstantiated loam and clay
Into a chancel where the choired birds sing

46

Green songs to golden god. The squirrels play
In ballet joy among the risen leaves;
The tomb of winter soughs with emptiness;
The visionary Adams and the Eves
Inhabit Eden of the new address.

And God looked down, and it was very good;
But here a bud was laggard, there a blade
Of grass, and in one foliating wood
Two lovers wore their coats. "Let there be shade,"
God said, and raised the sun by five degrees
To strip the lovers and to dress the trees.

3

All beds are preëxistent. Why should we
Exclaim to see the blankets and the sheet
And feel a mattress that we cannot see
Suspending us 'twixt heaven and earth? We meet
Because our mothers bore us. We were born
Because another father shaped this bed
In his carpentry shop, and, "Son," he said,
"An empty bed is frightfully forlorn."

So you and I were born, and here we are,
Gladly consenting to the father's will
Decreed before he built a trial-run star

(And when the novas splatter, binding still).
He who eternally begets his son
Made us a bed, made us, and made us one.

4

The massacre of solar hydrogen
To warm our blood is a mad, spendthrift thing.
In a system planned by provident men
Summer would be a lengthened name for spring;
The old wastrel, that sun, he would be rationed
In his consumption of his vital core
So a few extra centuries of us could be stationed
On the earth to shiver a few centuries more.

Still, sitting out here with you in the patio,
Naked as the neighbors up the hill will permit,
Inwardly, outwardly, dually aglow,
I'll let him squander the patrimony a bit
Of my blood claimants in the $n + n$ degree.
I'll never see them, and they'll never see me.

5

Hitchhikers are justified by faith through grace.
They do not work their way but wait their way
To the heavenly city. And the race

Is not always to the thumbs at dawn of day.
Many a thumb, at eventide extended,
Outdistances the prudent morning thumb.
This, in strict justice, cannot be defended,
But drivers deal the law of Kingdom Come.

The camera, my bank account, *Who's Who*
List no merits to claim you for my bed.
Faith rendezvoused with grace and I with you,
And good works followed, just as Luther said.
Here at the table, count them one by one:
Damaris, Madeline, Sarah, Alison.

6

Hide the broom in the rafters; your Dad's coming;
Submerge the empty cans into a box;
Flit the lone fly and still his lawless humming;
Tell Demie and Sarah to retrieve their sox.
There, good. I think the house will stand inspection,
And Dad can sink into the easy chair,
Open the *Times* and read the business section
And draw calm breaths of restful lakeside air.

Belovèd Eva, promise me you'll never
Iron the last shirt beneath the mounting pile;
I'll scatter ashes on the floor forever,

Write verse beneath a cobweb, yawn and smile.
Flit the hovering law and live by grace
And spare the rounded smoothness of your face.

7

You do not grow Euclidian but stranger,
Stranger than angels or the family cat.
You are the whirlpool, twister, every danger
Fantastic, real as a woman's hat.
Continents rise, descend, hover and break,
New oceans surge at newly modeled land.
Velikovsky's Venus left in her wake
Less carnage and creation than your hand.

Guided by burning bushes lit for us
On roads the Triple-A would not approve
Through deserts ominous and numinous
And seas that pant and part, by faith I move.
Though what and who you are I cannot know,
Safe in your danger, where you lead I go.

8

Earth we are of the earth. Then why not probe
Our mother matrix, seeking the lost gods,
Exiled, before the flood, inside this globe,

While our Yahweh equivocally nods?
We court lightning and a chaser of thunder;
God has green eyes; the Bible tells me so.
If we go under we may go back under.
In forty, fifty years we ought to know.

Meanwhile, let's say they're chthonic angels.
    Splendid!
Blind with long night, they've summoned us to find
The fruits and flowers they have blindly tended.
Better! I'll be the miner, you the mined.
I hear it's there the *blaue Blumen* grow,
And if I find them, I will tell you so.

9

I should have been a pair of ragged claws.
Perhaps I am. The shells and seaweed writhe
Like astigmatic lines of print. The laws
Of surface order snap. No tenth of tithe
Is offered to the god of sunlight here.
Here tooth and suckling tentacle compete;
All food is cannibal. Do not come near.
I dare not trust my eyesight when I eat.

I dare not trust, not trust, I must not trust.
And have I eaten apples in the light

And have I looked at balsam trees that thrust
Their Gothic spires into the ordered night?
Not night not day is this nor anything
That has a name where you sing where church bells
    ring.

10

Return, return, and turn to me again.
No, do not speak, our speaking did the harm.
I will be silent soon, and soon the pain
Of words will throb only. We shall disarm.
For in your arms, the only answer lies;
Words have betrayed us; we are words, words, words.
We is not found by multiplying *I's*.
In my redemption, nothing but the surds

Of your unreasoned breasts can make the sum
Of our one flesh, now hacked invisibly
But deep by words, words, words, that come,
Hypnotically spaced, from you, from me.
Rational numbers, rational words betray us.
The deaf night waits, and words shall not delay us.

11

As a communicant, past accidents

Of sense, knows, not believes, in bread and sips
Of wine his risen Lord in pledged descents
From heaven altarward and so to lips
Descends; yet knowing, longs to share That Day
When mercy's camouflage, like error, burns,
And Christ the judge the king the Z the A
In accident and substance joined, returns;

So I, upon the altar of this bed,
Knowing your naked body, know you veiled;
I take the sacramental wine and bread,
The substance, not the accidents, impaled.
Only That Day when wholly nude you shine
Will you be all men's, whole, and wholly mine.

12

We spat into the Yalu. Can you remember?
The splendid arrogance delights me still,
Now when the sudden Chinese of November
Blossom June mortars, hill to bloody hill.
Though the foxhole of our passion is frailly
Stout to resist the crawlers of the night,
We can recall the north, Manchuria palely
Infinite. We have seen beyond our sight.

Though now we look at maps, and 38

Is the straight line along the upper edge,
Though now our passion is to crouch and wait,
And horrors circle us at dusk, I pledge
We shall return, laugh by the Yalu, and spit,
Or fall, compass-north, pointing the road to it.

13

You are the contour map of God's creation.
A serious voyage from your hair to toes
Tenders a more progressive education
Than all the tools that Teacher's College knows.
Yea, though the rocket ships anchor on Venus
And televise their prospects to the earth,
The suns and planets made and laid between us
Are more extensive and of livelier worth.

Beyond the close domestic planets lie,
Millennial lighted, other universes,
Immune to men. Tom Corbett, thou shalt die
On Pluto's ignorant shores, light-made with curses.
But I in one night have winged the last extent
Of the curved cosmos through its sacrament.

14

With God all things are possible. Poor dancers

That we are—all careful one-two-three,
And one-two-three again, no splendid prancers
Or twirlers we—awkward and cautious we,
Ungraceful, tame, are not denied the grace
Of graceful God. For if we cannot waltz
Through gates of dance, there is the tortoise race
Won on slow knees. God pardons greater faults.

The blessèd angels wait for Arthur Murray
To shape the final glory of the dance.
The ballroom is prepared. We must not worry.
We, even we, will have our second chance.
The Trinity itself is never still.
Whoever comes to dance shall dance his fill.

15

As your light breath stirs and impedes my sleep,
As the iron of my hand to your magnetic
Side homes, my iconographic thoughts leap
To sea and ship soaring, sinking, frenetic
Unity of tempest and the lost. Sleep yet.
My hand rests peacefully upon your side.
I soon shall sleep, and in my breath no threat
Of hurricane will lash your quiet tide.

O ave carne, carne vale. We

Consumed the fat of Tuesday, now the ashes
Of Wednesday cross me, bless and darken me.
Your recent palms, burning, burnt, are the lashes
Of my patient passion, your lunar Lent,
The age but not the season of consent.

16

You dare not die before me. When you die
The stricken moon will plunge into the sea,
The anguished novas blaze the hurtling sky,
Scalded sea monsters writhe on quai and tree;
Blood will be sold in Coca-Cola bottles,
Babies offered to Moloch at High Mass,
Locomotives claim home rule for their throttles,
Sheep munch on flesh and panthers gorge on grass.

In you all things cohere, and their coherence
Is strong and frail as your sustaining heart.
Only you can veto Christ's new appearance
Set for That Day when the world falls apart.
I am unready. Spare the unready sky.
Lead me not into damnation. Do not die.

17

Shall I compare you to a marble plaque

And count the cycles rolling with your name?
No—dust and rain and war will summon back
The brief block letters playing hands with time.
And bronze, as staid as sin, will melt unlettered
In the atomic or the final fire.
All mortal monuments are nuptially fettered
Each to its ghost invisible and sure.

My words are writ on paper, not on stone,
And you will die and nourish grass and trees
Even as Helen, even as Héloïse.
Oh greet them kindly when the suns expire
Of pallor, and the molten marbles burn
To be your furnace and annealing fire.

18

When I am dead, mummify me no more
Than undertakers' lobbies and their laws
Require. Rip up the planks of an old pine floor,
Nail me a box, loose joined, so that the thaws
And freezes of my after years may enter
Without deceit and marry me again,
This time a woman, the symbiotic center
To taproots straight and masculine with rain.

Then, slowly rising through the greening stems

Of a deciduous shrub, may I bear flowers,
Bright, gay, to be my dancing requiems,
Immortally brief as these four girls of ours.
Thus marking time on some well-landscaped hill,
I'll be the parent of young daughters still.

19

We cannot plead compatibility
Before the judge. He is more modern than
A Broad Church bishop. His final decree
Is certain. Not husband and wife, but man
And woman enter heaven. O wife and lover,
In this brief paradise let us survey
The new found land of *Eros,* and discover
Its shyest cliffs and inlets. *Agapē*

The ocean will dissolve the continent,
Atlantis be a science-fiction fable.
And since my heart is nonetheless intent
On heaven, my mind is casually able
To know Lazarus was raised from the dead
And strange addition done with fish and bread.

20

When the unnatural warm fair October

Ended and a cold rain made the lawns muddy
Our vague disquiet ceased. Wintry and sober
We braced for snow, and weather-stripped the study.
But now the sun, blue sky, hot days returning
(November, though Wisconsin) we play young.
Dry leaves have no monopoly of burning.
Songs, decades forgotten, burn on my tongue.

One is always at home for what reprieves
The warden brings, nor does one controvert
The Governor's signature. Shakespearean leaves
Hang still in packets, and your April skirt
Is brighter than a hill of maple trees.
Unlike the doomed, we burn before we freeze.

21

I see you sitting in the easy chair,
The second cup of coffee at your right;
The lamp diffuses halos on your hair;
You are not made of atoms but of light.
Matter, I know from *Reader's Digest* science,
Is energy in a gregarious state,
And energy is light, you the appliance
That transmutes light and gives it shape and weight.

How great the condescension of your splendor

To mold the curving firmness of your cheek
And arms, and fingers tapering and tender,
And breasts and lips that listen, wait, and speak.
Love's appetite advances out of sight.
By alchemy five senses love the light.

22

To the left, cliffs; the shore where cottages
End with the road; mountain ascents of berries
For the valiant; antlers between the trees;
Tracks of a bear or two (the story varies).
To the right, fields studded with placid cows;
Fences in love with trees like English hedges;
Apple orchards with downward arching boughs;
Farm children diving from the low, bright ledges.

And we possess all shores as our canoe
Glides the long oval of the constant lake;
World upon world that folds into our view,
And fades like shifting bubbles in our wake.
We've made our choice for two abiding things:
Love and a lake refreshed by hidden springs.

23

After so many waves, after gray mountains

Undulating like playful mile-worms, after
Water that bobs me, drops me, sprays white fountains
Into my eyes and nose, after our laughter,
After the whorling meetings crest to crest,
Deterministic partings, words sea-drowned,
After the hour wind-blessed and wind-distressed,
Breathe deeply, plunge. It is time now for rest.

The turmoil of the wind is surface thin.
Down in the longing depth of quiet bronze
Only the sunlight follows from above.
I follow in the radiance of your skin.
Small fish swim parallel like boys in love;
The seaweed touches you with wistful fronds.

UNSCIENTIFIC POSTSCRIPT

The pseudoscientific say
It doesn't matter if you play
From dawn to dusk upon your cello,
Its tones will not become more mellow.

They do not know, but lovers know
That use refines body and bow
Till both respond with one intent
To song that wants embodiment.

The lightest lips upon your breast
And Amor incarnatus est.
My bow against the vibrant strings,
The cosmos in my cello sings.

THE VERTICAL MOMENT

Karl Barth went strolling down the lunar valley,
The pipe of nature fuming from his teeth.
The night was graceless as a city alley,
The fallen lava hinted hell beneath.

"I am so damned, completely damned," he sang,
And struck a match to light his pipe again,
And then, in the instant glow, he saw It hang—
Shadow of Grace, light-year extended—then—

"Holy, holy, holy," and he was silent;
His knees bruised the porous veneer of stone;
The Trinity raged through his body in violent
Ballet. And once more Karl Barth was alone.

"Holy, holy, holy," he told the night,
Picked up his pipe, and fumbled for a light.

WHEN THE WORLD DROWNED
for Chomingwen Pond, upon her baptism

When the world drowned, it was your splendid guilt.
The font could not contain the weight of carnage.
The marble shattered, and the water spilt

(Water that, overflowing, rises faster)
Over the pews, the Andes, and the Alps.
And Noah did not float out this disaster.

Dead bodies rode the universal sea,
Rotating silent in the local whirlpools,
A thousand fathoms over the highest tree.

And sin, once called original (now standard
As the pale verse of Eliot's epigones)
Raged in the Bendix of the sea, was laundered

To apple red, the red of Abel's blood.
Colors at last were plainly separated,
And nothing was the color now of mud.

My body floated with the silent others.
I think I touched you in your lovely death.
All men were water-gone, all men were brothers.

When the first olive leaf awoke my skin,
When roses mounted through the dying water,
And the green world surged to the scarlet sun,

The live men frolicked in their ghostly freedom.
We danced with preëxistent unicorns,
Took bread and wine, and I was new as Adam.

THE WHIRLPOOL OUT OF TIME

1   The Garden of Common Sense

For $2 + 2$ is 4, and H + O
Gives H_2O, and if I speak of water,
Evoking memories of cool spray blown
Off mountain waterfalls, and drops that spatter
In transient silver from the brimming bucket,
Remember that the peasant word denotes
No more than H_2O; the dewdrop on the thicket
A billion solar systems called a globe.

Shun the square root of —1, or Jeans
Will twirl the microscope and show you Plato.
Protect your physics from a prefix. Read
Euclid each night before retiring. Veto
The *i* (italicized). Plain I is ample
(Capitalized) to meet your needs. You need
To   quench   your   thirst   with   canned   milk.   Life   is
      simple.
And alcohol will wash your body clean.

I saved up string and match-sticks in my youth
Until I had a notable collection.

I'll diagram a theorem or two
Now in the quiet, when the dull distraction
Of rain has ended, ending thoughts of Helen.
Here is the square on the hypotenuse,
And equal to the sum. A sparrow's fallen.
It's dead, it's dead, and pity 'tis 'tis true.

2   Rain, Rain, Go Away

My arm was hygienic when I bought it
At Kresge's, sealed in virgin cellophane.
I wonder why the roaches want to eat it.
This curious patch of gray or greenish gray
Above the wrist was smaller yesterday,
But yesterday the sun was brightly shining.
If I could twist the faucet of the rain,
But that demands research and further planning.

The rain beats down, breeding fungus on wounded
Bark and defective skin, chilling the trees
And me, bearing the loosened leaf upended
To shroud the fallen sparrow; slithers, seeps
Below the mold's cosmetic face, keeps
A rendezvous with rotting roots and sockets
Forlorn of eyes, and whitening hands that reach
Into the midnight of inverted thickets.

67

I dreamed last night about a lovely forest.
The soil was made of concrete, tinted dun;
Trunks and branches, aluminum; the clearest
Of crystal globes, fashioned in clusters, hung
In the bright sun, filled with synthetic pulp
Of every fruit. The tinfoil leaves could flutter
But never fall. I'll hang my arm upon
A Judas tree but not go near the water.

3   The Meditation of the Roots

Why are the dead so slow to learn to die?
Surely by now they know that deep, far deeper
Than six feet lies the death that they desire.
Alas that they were laid to face the upper
Turmoil of broken roots and loosened pebbles
And be betrayed by filtered flecks of light.
The way to death is downward, past the fables
Of memory to silence, depth, and night.

But night by night we feel the piteous strength
Of withered fingers grasping, bodies writhing,
Bequeathing us their slowly parted flesh,
Till they are free, vague shapes of white and
        loathing,
To wander from forsaken cemeteries,

68

Clutching the children of remembered friends,
Stopping strangers with incoherent stories,
Peering through blinds at ancient nuptial beds.

We have a legend of an apple tree
Whose roots possessed the gift of prophesying.
They said, One man shall briefly rest between
The restless dead, and then, with eyes, full-seeing,
Turn downward, grapple with the stubborn inches
To depth and death and truly die; and we,
Escorted by the dead, will follow; kin and branches
Renounced for a dead man. But where is he?

4   A Place of Skulls

The forest of my dream was not as lovely.
Blanched bone is brighter than aluminum.
The spinal columns and the limbs are bravely
Bearing aloft their clustered fruit of skulls
To gleam with iridescence in the sun.
And see my white arm where I left it hanging.
Its finger bones are strong. From each is hung
A swaying sphere to set the breezes singing.

I'll count them. One, two, three, four, five, six, seven.
That can't be right. My fingers came to five.
One skull per finger. One, two, three, four. Even

This time. And 2 + 2 is 4. My eyes
Are 20/20. One, two, four, ten, five.
No, no. I think that someone made an error
In subtraction, and Euclid drew a line
Unknowing. I the heir. And 0 the horror.

I am weary with sums, and I am hungry.
These clusters edge my teeth, like chalk on slate.
I am thirsty. I wish that I were angry
At empty spheres. If there were pools of rain
I would kneel down and press my lips—my face,
Reflected there—white, bright? No lips to hamper
Teeth of uncertain count? This is the way
The world ends. Not with a bang but a simper.

5   He Descended

From where he stood, this little spot of earth
Circled in space, a child's top slowly spinning.
His father saw it, too, but spoke no word.
The word he uttered leaped. It started raining.
The long spears of the rain were his companions
Over the wine-dark sea, past Rome astir
And Athens deep in optional opinions
Until he found the place to do his work.

And he descended to the shallow dead.

"Go back, go back!" they mourned. "You cannot
  save us.
Here each must scale to sunlight by himself.
You are so lightly dead. Leap back and leave us."
He saw the pale twigs of their fingers thrusting
In palisades above the structural heads.
He softly swerved the bones of their resisting
And spoke once. "Follow me." He followed death.

He followed death into the depth and dark
Where taproots end and stone in twisted layers
Yields sullen crevices to bleeding arms
And rationed breath for thinly scattered prayers.
He found death in the phosphorescent whirlpool
Rotating counter-earthwise at the heart
Of earth. The drowned man eddied in the pale pool
Until a current bore him very far.

6   The Song of the Sparrow

With a last failure of my twitching feathers
I left my body on the fallen leaves
And time consumed it with the numbered others
In chemistry to hold the forest green.
And yet, time stopped. How that can be—I mean—
My years had been a sparrow's, days of barely

Enough of sun for careless grain and seeds—
No hours to win the words to say this clearly—

And yet, time stopped, and in the silenced moment
That had no breadth (for time had stopped) I knew
Beyond all haggling of reward and payment
No fixed decree in catalytic roots.
And when my wings, feathered in light, rose, flew
In a sure spiral to this morning meeting—
All changed, changed utterly, all things anew,
In forest, feathers, and the final mating—

But what is new? The glory or my vision?
And was I always where I have not been?
What was the moment of the planned invasion?
I think that I must think of many things.
For there is time, fullness of time, to think,
And time to greet the sparrow hawk, my brother,
Veering to me on swift and ah! bright wings
Beneath the dove who wills our wings together.

7   A Terrible Beauty Is Born

Here is a nightmare or a fairy tale
Or both, with drawings by the wilder Dali.
Black roots and whitened dead descend like rain;
Above my skull the rain is beating dully.

For I have seen him, I have heard him speaking
To me among the dead men when he came
All in a bitter passion of forsaking
To teach me mathematics and a name,

To lead me to the end of Mazda lights
Into the pure geometry of drowning.
And here's a farewell to a sullen eye.
One way, one eye. The son of light is reigning
Over dark depths, the huntsman and the hunted,
O fell me to the whirlpool out of time
(For this is what the rain and sparrow hinted)
And drown me out of death into your life.

The word I could not speak is uttered now
For me and utterly informs the silence,
For 1 + 1 + 1 is 1, and round
The honest lines that Euclid brings to balance,
Beyond the newer space of final curving,
Beneath the wistful roots, and in a drowned
Man's heart (my heart) the word: forgiving, living,
Giving. I did not find you. I was found.

GEOGRAPHICAL NOTE

The rather numerous geographical allusions in this book will be clarified if the reader bears in mind that most of them refer to one or another of four areas:

(1) Beloit, a small city in southern Wisconsin.

(2) Lake Iroquois (Hinesburg Pond), south of Burlington, Vermont.

(3) Talpa, a Spanish-speaking village near Taos, New Mexico.

(4) Corte Madera, a suburb a few miles north of San Francisco. It commands a good view of both San Quentin and Mount Tamalpais, the latter being the highest mountain in the region. Anyone driving from San Francisco crosses the magnificent and beautiful Golden Gate Bridge, with a view of Alcatraz to the right.

Nearly all the remaining geographical references presuppose nothing more than an ordinary familiarity with the Bible, science fiction, history, and newspaper headlines.

—C. W.

Set in Intertype Garamond
Format by Robert Cheney
Manufactured by The Haddon Craftsmen, Inc.
Published by HARPER & BROTHERS, *New York*